Designed by Flowerpot Press
www.FlowerpotPress.com
CHC-0909-0582
ISBN: 978-1-4867-2416-1
Made in China/Fabriqué en Chine

Have you ever wanted to buy that extra cookie at school? What about that new book your sister really wants for her birthday? It can be great having your own money to spend however you want, and it is even better knowing that you earned it all on your own!

So on to the real question...

How do kids just like you make money? Do they draw George Washington's face on green pieces of paper?

No way! You can earn money by starting your own business or getting a job in your neighborhood. Let's learn some kid-friendly ways to earn some money.

Mom and Dad, I need advice!

DON'T FORGET

When considering ways to make money it is important to talk to a parent or guardian first! Not only should you get their permission, but they may also have helpful advice to get you started!

SELLING THINGS

How do you make money selling lemonade? Do you go back in time and invent lemonade then sell the idea for millions of dollars?

No way! Making money is tough enough without having to bring time travel into it!

You can make money by starting a lemonade stand or selling baked goods. Who doesn't love a refreshing glass of lemonade or a delicious chocolate cupcake?

GOOD TIP

A good way to attract lots of customers is by having as many options as possible. Try offering a sugar-free lemonade option or different varieties of baked goods that can accommodate allergies or restrictions.

I can't wait to try the lemonade!

Follow these steps to start your lemonade stand business.

Step 1: Create a plan for your business. Your business plan will outline what your goals are, what you plan to sell, and how you plan to do it.

chocolate chip cookies

+ sugar

+ water

= lemonade

lemons

cupcakes

cookies

Step 2: Gather supplies and make your product. Your product is what you plan to sell, for example, your lemonade and cookies.

Step 3: Create a poster advertising your business and the price of your products.

PRICE LIST

LEMONADE.............................$0.50
COOKIE...................................$1.00
CUPCAKE................................$1.50

FUN FACT
The earliest lemonade stand was in 1873!

4

FRESH LEMONADE

fresh lemons

Step 4: Find a place to set up your business. Make sure you gather what you need and get permission before setting up.

Step 5: Serve your community with a great attitude! Customers return to businesses where they have good experiences, so make sure to be extra nice and helpful to anyone who buys from you.

5

Fresh-squeezed lemonade!

Let's talk money...

When you are gathering supplies for your products, be sure to calculate how much money you need to earn for the business to be successful. For example, if you spent $20 on supplies, then you will want to make more than $20 in sales to make money for you to keep. Knowing how much your supplies cost will help you know how to price your products.

Thank you for your support!

TAKING CARE

How do you make money by house sitting for a neighbor? Do you set up a telescope so you can watch their front door from your room?

No way! It's easy to help your neighbors or friends when they go out of town— no telescope needed.

Don't worry, Mr. Green! I'll take care of things. Have a great trip!

What are you doing?

Just keeping an eye on Mr. Green's house!

There are several ways to help out a neighbor while they are on vacation. You can help by taking care of their pets, taking out the trash and recycling, bringing the mail inside, watering plants, or just checking in on the house from time to time to make sure everything is ok.

Let's talk money...

Discuss a rate with your customer based on the number of days you will be helping and the number of tasks you are being asked to help out with. Usually, the more you do, the more you can earn.

GOOD TIP

Consider doing something extra to help your business stand out. You can offer to help with laundry, clean the house, or leave flowers to surprise them upon their arrival home. Going the extra mile will never hurt you and most of the time it will result in a returning customer which is key for a successful business!

Welcome home! Hope you had a great trip!

Great work! Thanks so much!

SUMMER CAMP FOR KIDS

Are you sure this is a good idea?

How do you make money by babysitting? Do you start a summer camp at your house and invite all the kids in the neighborhood?

No way! Better to start with one family at a time!

Babysitting is a great way to make a little extra money, even if you may not be ready to babysit all on your own. Offering to help around the house or babysit with parental support nearby is a great start. Watching the kids allows parents to do daily chores, work from home, or just take a break and relax, all while knowing their kids are safe and having fun in their own home!

Whether it is house sitting, pet sitting, or babysitting, building relationships is important. Showing your interest in the job by offering a free trial, spending extra time learning what the customer needs, and showing up prepared and on time goes a long way and can ensure customers stick with you for a long time.

Let's talk money...

Determining a rate for your services can be helpful when meeting with a customer for the first time. It is important to discuss expectations in the beginning and be open to changes in your rate based on what the customer expects, how frequently you work with that customer, and your level of experience.

We can make a lot of money, my friend!

LAWN CARE

How do you make money mowing the lawn? Do you get a bunch of goats to come eat all the grass in your neighbors' yards?

No way! You don't need goats to help you make money.

You can just offer simple lawn care services to your neighbors and friends using what you already have. You can mow the lawn, rake leaves, plant flowers, lay mulch, trim bushes, or pull weeds. You can even make some extra money in the winter months by offering to shovel snow.

Before starting your lawn care business, you will want to start by advertising your services. You can do this in many ways. You can advertise your services by using social media (with permission and supervision from a guardian or parent), hanging flyers around your neighborhood, or sending e-mails or letters to neighbors in your area.

GOOD TIP

Once you start to get customers, you want to make sure that you know exactly what they want and how they want it. This builds a trust with your customer and they will know that you have their best interest in mind. Customer loyalty is a very big part of running a successful business!

Let's talk money...

Different jobs may earn you different amounts of money. Your experience level and how frequently you visit your customer could play a part in how much they are willing to pay for your services. If you need tools to do the job, keep in mind you will have to calculate that into how much money you make. You can always ask to borrow any tools until you are able to buy your own.

CLEANING SERVICES

How do you make money by washing cars? Do you turn on all the sprinklers on your street and ask people to drive back and forth?

No way! You don't want to accidentally flood your street!

Washing cars or even bikes is a really simple way to make money. Many people want others to wash their stuff for them so that they don't have to do it themselves! All you need is access to a hose, soap, a towel, and a cleaning tool, such as a sponge. Once you get your supplies, you are ready to go!

GOOD TIP

Picking a good location for your car wash is important. You want to find a place that cars can easily get in and out of and an area with plenty of room for your supplies and access to water. Asking permission to use a parking lot or asking your neighbors to use a small section of your street are both good options!

shampoo

water

large towel

hair dryer

tub

brush

Cars aren't the only thing you can wash to make a little extra money. Offering dog bathing services is another fun way to start a business and spend time with some adorable furry friends. Just like washing a car, you need supplies, such as shampoo, a tub or access to water, towels, and brushes.

Let's talk money...

You may choose to charge a base rate for the dogs or cars you wash, but you can also determine different rates if the dog or car is bigger or smaller.

TECH SUPPORT

How do you make money using your smartphone, tablet, or computer?
Do you contact all your friends and ask them for $20?

No way! You can actually help other people use their phones and technology
to earn extra money without pestering your friends.

Technology is rapidly growing and evolving every day! That is why tech support is a very smart way to make some money. Younger generations are known to be more advanced with technology because they have grown up with it their whole life.

You can help your customers with tech support by writing notes or specific steps for them to follow in case they need your help when you aren't around. You can also offer to help set up new technology or even show them new ways to use the technology they already have.

Let's talk money...

You can make money with your tech knowledge by offering to do a tech seminar in your neighborhood and charging a small fee or offering to do a couple hours of tech work for a reasonable rate. Check out some of these ideas!

WAYS YOU CAN HELP!

Delete unwanted pictures and videos

Help gather and organize friends, family, and favorites contact lists

Help clean out e-mail inboxes

Delete unwanted data or organize apps, photos, and documents

FUN FACT
In the US, over 150 million strands of lights are sold each year around the holiday season!

HOLIDAY HELPER
How do you make money around the holidays? Do you display decorations on your grumpy neighbor's lawn for them to find in the morning?

No way! You probably wouldn't want to surprise them with lawn art, especially if they didn't ask for it!

Putting up holiday lights and decorations is a great way to earn extra money, especially since there are so many holidays to offer your services for. If you are wanting recurring business, then be sure to call your customer before every holiday and ask if they need help decorating for the occasion. Showing your customer that you are thinking of them and their satisfaction is a great way to keep your customers happy and will encourage them to spread the word about your services.

Let's talk money...

Seasonal jobs can sometimes be less reliable but in many ways can be more desirable. Finding the right people and asking for a reasonable rate is the key to keeping seasonal customers. And in most cases, you won't need to provide the decorations, so the money you make goes straight to you!

MONEY MANAGEMENT

You've made some money with your awesome business ideas, now what? Learning what to do with your money is important. You can spend it or you can save it or you can donate it. Even better, you can do all three! Here are some money management tips and good habits for you to develop as you continue to grow your business and make money.

IF YOU WANT TO SPEND...

Buying something you have had your eye on is always a lot of fun! You should be able to spend the money you earn on things you enjoy, but it is important to be mindful of your spending.

TIP #1

Know the value of the things you want to buy. Fully understanding how much something costs is important. Sometimes the number you see isn't the final amount you will pay. Be sure you have enough money to cover the cost of the item you want to buy and any additional fees or taxes.

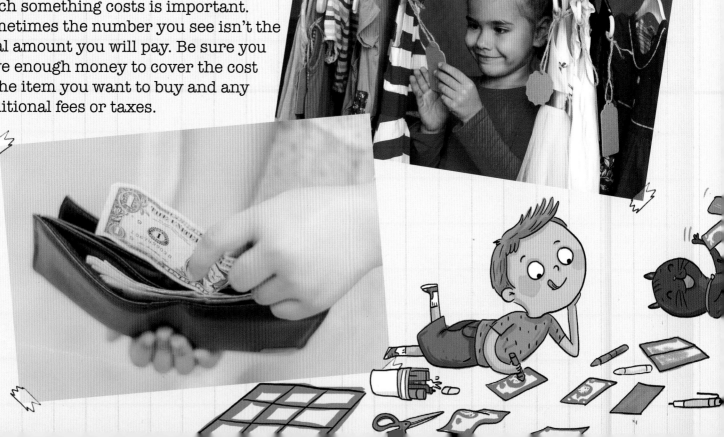

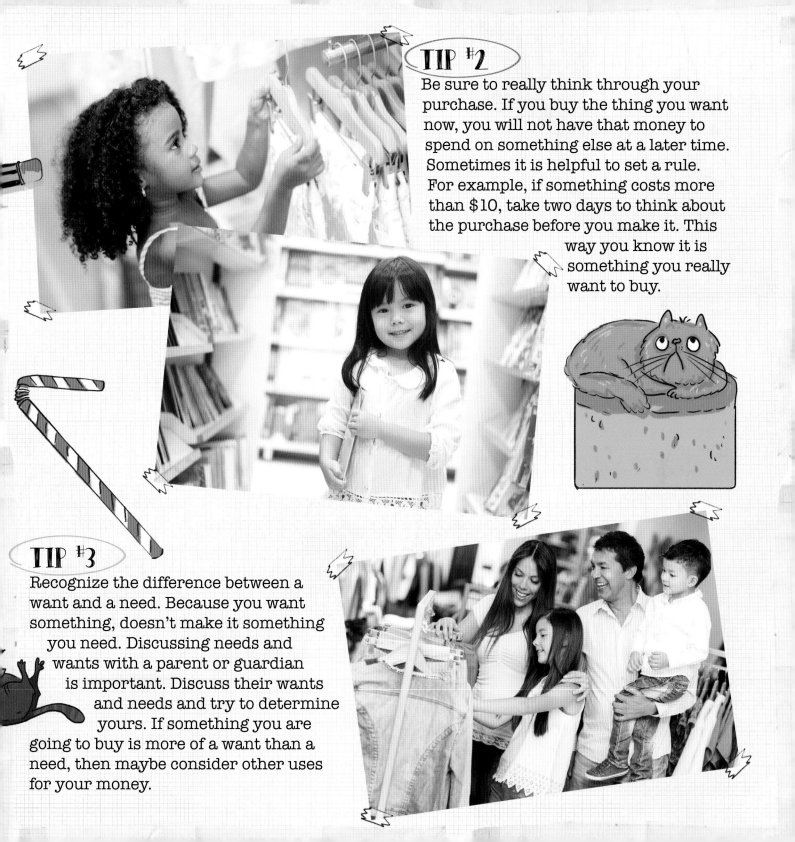

TIP #2

Be sure to really think through your purchase. If you buy the thing you want now, you will not have that money to spend on something else at a later time. Sometimes it is helpful to set a rule. For example, if something costs more than $10, take two days to think about the purchase before you make it. This way you know it is something you really want to buy.

TIP #3

Recognize the difference between a want and a need. Because you want something, doesn't make it something you need. Discussing needs and wants with a parent or guardian is important. Discuss their wants and needs and try to determine yours. If something you are going to buy is more of a want than a need, then maybe consider other uses for your money.

IF YOU WANT TO SAVE...

Saving your money is a great option, and starting to save money early is even better! The goal of saving is to leave the money you earn alone until you need it or you have met your savings goal.

TIP #1

Find a safe and secure place to keep your money. Some people like piggy banks, while others like clear jars so they can see their money add up. Whatever you choose, make sure you collect all your earnings in one place.

TIP #2

Set a goal! If you are saving up for something special or just putting money away for a later need, it is helpful to determine how much money you want to save and how long it will take you to save it. Keep track of your goal by writing down each time you put money into your savings. Once you reach your goal, try setting an even higher one!

TIP #3

Set some money aside for savings every single time you earn it. If you plan to take a small fraction of the money you earn and place it into your savings, that money will grow! Forming a habit of putting money into your piggy bank will get easier over time and set you up for future success.

TIP #4

If you fill up your jar, you can ask a parent or guardian to help you open a bank account. A bank account is a safe place to store your money and in some cases a way to help you earn even more.

IF YOU WANT TO SHARE...

The third thing you can do with your money is give to charities or organizations that are important to you. For example, if you love animals, you can donate some of your money to help animals at the local animal shelter. There are lots of places to donate and any amount helps!

TIP #1

Find something you love! There are so many organizations out there to help people and animals in need. Use your interests and hobbies to help you find places that will accept donations.

TIP #2

Set up a giving jar. Just like a savings jar, a giving jar can be a place where you set aside a small amount of money to go to the charity of your choosing.

TIP #3

Giving money isn't the only way to share. Buying a toy for a toy drive or ingredients to make cookies for a bake sale is also another form of donating using the money you have earned.

BUDGETING

A helpful and easy way to keep track of your money is to make a budget. A budget tells you what you are earning, saving, spending, and giving. Take a look at the sample budget below and learn more about what goes in each column of your budget.

DATE	DESCRIPTION	EARN	SPEND	SAVE	SHARE	BALANCE
10/5	Money from dog sitting	$25.00				$25.00
10/8	Ice cream from the ice cream truck		$5.00			$20.00
10/8	Savings for the book fair			$5.00		$15.00
10/20	Money for the bake sale				$10.00	$5.00

The DATE column helps you keep track of when you earned or spent your money.

The DESCRIPTION column tells you what your money was spent on or what you saved it for. Your description can be as simple or as detailed as you want!

The EARN column is where you keep track of the money you have made from completing a job.

The SPEND column is where you keep track of the money you used to buy something.

The SAVE column is where you keep track of the money you put away in your piggy bank or savings jar.

The SHARE column is where you keep track of the money you donated.

The BALANCE column is where you keep track of the total amount of money you have to spend. As you earn or spend money, you will add or subtract your total in the balance column to keep track of the money you have at any given time.